JOAN MANNING-SANDERS

A YOUNG ARTIST

JOAN MANNING-SANDERS

JOAN MANNING-SANDERS

A YOUNG ARTIST

※

WITH AN INTRODUCTION BY

HELEN FERRIS

NEW YORK

THE JUNIOR LITERARY GUILD

1931

PLATES PRINTED IN GREAT BRITAIN
BY CHARLES WHITTINGHAM & GRIGGS, LTD.
TYPOGRAPHY BY THE PRINTING HOUSE OF
WILLIAM EDWIN RUDGE

PUBLISHED IN AMERICA
BY
WILLIAM EDWIN RUDGE

JOAN MANNING-SANDERS

By Helen Ferris

IT WAS a June afternoon in London and the long art gallery was filled with men and women eagerly looking at the pictures hung on the walls. For these pictures had a very special interest. Each had been painted by a young artist. And the widely announced exhibition, which had been organized by *The Daily Express,* had brought together the work of many young English men and women.

Of all the pictures there, two attracted special attention that day of the opening —*The Pedlar* and *David and the Globe*. Caught by the unusual quality in the painting, the visitors consulted their catalogues. Who was the artist?

"Joan Manning-Sanders," they read. "Aged eighteen."

Looking again at the pictures there before them, they were amazed. Only eighteen!

Their amazement grew when they later learned that a mistake had been made in the catalogue. Joan Manning-Sanders was thirteen, not eighteen, they were told. The figure "3" upon the entry blank had been read as an "8."

But the most interesting part of the whole story is that if this mistake and one other had not been made, Joan's pictures would not have appeared in the Young Artists' Exhibition at all. For the Exhibition, as announced, was open only to those between the ages of eighteen and forty. Joan, being thirteen, would not have been eligible.

And this is what had happened. Miles away from London, in a small fishing hamlet called Sennen Cove, tucked away under high cliffs known as Land's End, Joan was hard at work finishing two pictures when news of the Exhibition reached her. One of the pictures which she was painting was an oil portrait of a Cornishman who went from door to door in that part of the country, selling his assorted wares. The other was of her brother David at work on his home lessons.

Excitedly reading the announcement, noticing only that she barely had time to put the last touches upon the portraits and get them to London, Joan did not read the Exhibition entry rules carefully. She did not even see that only those of eighteen or more were eligible. Hastily filling out the forms which were to accompany all pictures sent for approval to the Young Artists' Exhibition, she serenely entered her age as thirteen, and was overjoyed when she heard that both *The Pedlar* and *David and the Globe* had been accepted.

When, later, Joan's friends called the attention of the Exhibition Committee to the mistake that had been made, Joan's entry blank was brought out and examined. Yes, there was "13" quite unmistakably. The Committee, too, had made a mistake.

But no one was sorry. The Exhibition's many visitors continued to enjoy Joan's pictures. Art critics, writing of the painting exhibited there, praised what she had done. And a thirteen-year-old girl at Land's End was encouraged to continue with the work which meant so much to her.

"Who is she?" people asked. "And how has it happened that she can paint so beautifully?"

When Joan Manning-Sanders was born at Tor Cross in South Devon, England, on May seventeenth, 1913, everyone who knew her father and mother felt certain that here was a baby girl who would grow up into an interesting or perhaps even an unusual young woman. For her father was George Manning-Sanders, whose exquisite short stories had already attracted the attention of those who appreciate fine writing, and her mother was Ruth Manning-Sanders, a poet and novelist of distinction—two writers, who cared so much for beauty that until Joan was born they lived in a caravan, going from place to place in England's beautiful countryside.

After Joan and her brother, David, two years younger, joined them, the caravan was impractical, but even then the Manning-Sanders family did not settle down for years. They lived in Bude and Newlyn in Cornwall, in Midhurst in Sussex, in Catchal in Cornwall, in Grasse behind Cannes in France, back again in Catchal, and then in Sennen Cove near Land's End!

From her babyhood, Joan loved the out-of-doors. She was never far from fields and hills and birds and trees and flowers. The people of hamlets and villages were her friends. And from the time she was nine until she was thirteen, there was always her horse, Tom, waiting for her in the stable. Wherever she lived, the sight of Joan on Tom, riding alone along country roads and followed by the family's large black dog, Luck, was a familiar sight.

8

What with living in Bude and Newlyn and Midhurst and Catchal and Grasse, the best kind of school for Joan and David seemed to be one that would go along with them. And no part of her childhood remains more vivid to Joan, or more delightful, than her hours with Miss Florence Bridge, their governess, whom the family affectionately called "Bridget."

It was Miss Bridge who first suggested that Joan and David make pictures of the events in their history books and the Bible stories which so interested them. When they did not know what costumes the people of those days wore—and so could not draw them—she sent Joan and David to the library to look up reference books which would give them the information they needed. When the trees and the hills and the flowers of their pictures looked queer, she suggested that they take their drawing pads and pencils outdoors and draw from nature.

The first seven pictures in this book are some of those which Joan thus drew in colored chalk for Miss Bridge—*Adam and Eve, The Israelites Marching Round the Walls of Jericho, Joseph Going to Bury His Father, The Egyptians Pursuing the Israelites through the Red Sea, King David Dancing Before the Ark, The Death of Absalom,* and *Elijah and the Flaming Altar*—all of them done before she was twelve.

When, later, a friend asked her about these pictures, she said, "For the Jericho costumes, we went to the library. For the Joseph picture, David and Bridget and I made cardboard models of the Egyptian chariots. I copied the trees in the Ark picture from one just outside our garden. I made the mule look sly because I thought that, being a mule, he had done it on purpose. And I drew the faces in the Elijah picture out of my head and hated them afterward."

Until she was eleven, drawing pictures was to Joan simply one of many interesting things to do. She and her brother David used to take long country walks together, often coming home with a wounded bird or animal which they had picked up and which they cared for until it was well again—or, as sometimes unfortunately happened, until it died.

It was in this way that Joan made an amusing pet of a carrion crow, which she found one evening under a tree and which looked as if it had been trampled upon. The crow recovered, but when given its freedom refused to leave. And although it was allowed to fly wherever it wished, for two years it always returned to the family where it was an amusing, mischievous pet. He roosted outside Joan's window, tapping on the pane with his bill in the night, to wake her up. He tormented Luck, flying off with his ball or his best bone and imitating his bark in a most maddening way. Perched on the branch of a tree over the road, the madcap delighted in setting up a sudden terrific clatter at the surprised farmers who were driving below. And once he drove a herd of cows home an hour before milking time by strutting after them, barking.

When Joan and her family moved to Sennen Cove, the crow went along, but he disappeared when Joan happened to be away for a short visit. Before he left, however, he had served as model in many of Joan's pictures and you will find his portrait—"though slightly enlarged to raven proportions," as Joan's mother says—in the unfinished painting of the skull and bird in this book.

As soon as she could read, books were another of Joan's loves. From the time she was seven, she was an eager reader of poetry, and later of Chaucer, Milton, Dostoyevsky, Jane Austen and as many nature books as she could find. As a small girl, she was especially interested in the writings of Fabre and following some chance suggestion of his, she started collecting the skulls of birds and animals which she came upon in her rambles through the fields and woods. The delicacy and intricacy of the bone structure fascinated her. She spent hours polishing them and often said it was a pity that anything so marvelous had to be covered with flesh. Without realizing it, small Joan was acquiring something which every portrait painter needs—a knowledge of anatomy.

And so, what with lessons and rambles and drawing and reading and riding and collecting, Joan reached her eleventh birthday. The pictures which she drew were still only an amusing pastime to her. Her family, too, saw in them nothing more than excellent childish efforts which were to be encouraged chiefly because Joan was so interested in them.

But the year she was eleven, something happened which was to change Joan's life from then on. A friend of Mr. Manning-Sanders, Father Bernard Walke of St. Hilary Church in Cornwall, came to visit them. Looking at the chalk drawings which Joan had made for Miss Bridge, he was at once impressed with their unusual quality. And to the family's surprise, he asked Joan to paint a series of six water color pictures of the childhood of Christ, for his church.

Joan accepted the commission and set to work. No subject could have been given her in which she would have had a deeper interest. Nor could any encouragement have been greater than the belief of her older friend that she was able to paint pictures which he would wish to have in his own church.

But even so, it was a difficult task for an eleven-year-old. What scenes from the story of Christ's childhood should she select? What people should be in them? What about the landscape background? So much to be decided before she could even start!

Today, in St. Hilary Church in Cornwall, visitors find Joan Manning-Sanders' six paintings—*A King Following the Star of Bethlehem, The Flight into Egypt, An Angel Appearing to the Shepherds, The Annunciation, The Glorification,* and *The Adoration of the Kings.*

Joan's mother and father, Miss Bridge and David know with what care Joan planned and painted each picture. They know of the long hours of work during the year before the series was finished. For Joan was determined not only to have each picture as a whole as beautiful in design and conception as she could make it, she wished to have each small part of each picture accurate. Before she painted any object or animal or person into the larger picture, she made separate sketches of every one, working upon it until she felt able to use it. And just as in the pictures she had made for Miss Bridge, she had used the trees and the flowers around her, so now Joan painted the stone walls and the pleasant hills of the Cornish countryside into her Bible scenes. You will find them, if you look, in the first three of the St. Hilary paintings reproduced in this book—*A King Following the Star of Bethlehem, The Flight into Egypt,* and *An Angel Appearing to the Shepherds.*

And her father and mother and David and Tom and Luck and the crow were most useful. Her mother sat on Tom, as the model for the legs of the King in the *King Following the Star* picture and delights in telling how Joan, who had imagined the king's legs as being straight down from the saddle, was extremely annoyed when her model sat in the saddle with normally bent knees! Finally, Joan drew the feet in the stirrups only, and held to her conception of the rigid legs—all of which is in the picture, as you see. Mr. Manning-Sanders sat as model for Joseph's hands in *The Flight into Egypt.* Luck was coaxed to stand for the dog which is being led by the attendant following the king in the first of the St. Hilary paintings. Tom is the horse in the same painting. And the pet crow of the family is standing on the well in the picture of *The Adoration*. David, too, acted as model, although a rather restless one.

And so, at last, the six pictures were completed. Not to Joan's entire satisfaction, however. Even after Father Walke accepted them with delight, there remained much that Joan wished she might improve in them. They were, to be sure, the best work of which she was then capable. What Joan wished, however, was that she were capable of more.

But to anyone who compares her picture of *Adam and Eve*, the first in this book, drawn when she was eight, with *The Adoration*, the last of the St. Hilary pictures, painted when she was eleven, the wonder is that in three short years, without any art training, she could have gone so far.

Her work upon the series brought Joan far more than the praise of Father Walke and the others who first saw the pictures. Joan now knew what she wished to do. The family plan for her and David had been St. George's School, at Harpenden. Joan's new plan did not include St. George's. She wished to remain at home and paint. And because Mr. and Mrs. Manning-Sanders were themselves artists, painting pictures in words, because they knew the years of effort necessary to anyone, however talented, who wishes to go forward toward his dream, they recognized the significance of Joan's decision and desire.

So David went away to St. George's without Joan. And Joan was given her first studio, so near the sea that at high tide it is possible to throw a stone into the water, and where boats to and from America pass by each day. Here she worked with her first oil paints. Here, at her easel, she started upon pictures of what she herself saw, day by day, instead of scenes she imagined from her books. The sketch of David which follows the St. Hilary paintings in this book was her first step in this experimenting. And it is interesting to know that she was at work upon it even before she had completed the water color series.

The other pictures which follow here in the book were all painted by Joan in her Sennen Cove studio before she was sixteen. And nothing could be written about her which would tell more about the things which interest her than the subjects which she chooses for her pictures. The people of the countryside—the pedlar at the door, farmers with their horses at a ploughing contest, three fishermen at their game of checkers, children, a group of Cornishmen with their concertinas, harmonica and flute. And the fields and the hills and the hedges and the winding little roads. These are the people whom Joan knows in her small fishing hamlet. This is the country she loves.

Painting the folk about her, she seems able deftly to catch upon her canvas the special thing in each person which makes him an individual. Painting the Cornish countryside, she conveys through the color and design of her pictures the distinctive quality which makes the Cornish landscape different from any other.

It was to this reality in Joan's paintings that those who attended the opening of the Young Artists' Exhibition quickly responded that day in London. *A Pedlar* —so real that one can imagine his coming up to one's own door and displaying his oddments. *David and the Globe*—just such a picture as many a father and mother have seen at their own library table during homework time.

Yes, the people Joan paints are real people to her, not simply models she has chosen for her pictures. And while she is deeply gratified that her *Pedlar* picture was so favorably received at her first exhibition, and while she is justly proud that her picture *The Brothers* was accepted for exhibition at the Royal Academy, what she will tell you of these pictures, if you mention them to her, is amusing stories about the pedlar himself and the three brothers.

This is the story of the pedlar, over which she chuckles. It seems that when Joan's pictures were exhibited in the Young Artists' Exhibition, the painting of *The Pedlar* was photographed and reproduced in many newspapers. Whereupon the model, Mr. William Dungey, the pedlar himself, became something of a Cornish celebrity. He had grumbled very much at having to sit so still while his portrait was being painted and had refused to take off his hat or to part with his iron-shod walking stick. But as soon as the portrait was published, he began to boast at every door of what a handsome man he was. For according to his reasoning, he *must* be handsome, otherwise his portrait would not be attracting so much attention!

His customers, however, refused to be convinced. Whereupon, he changed his story and boasted of his very fine complexion. For a long time he journeyed to the artists' colonies at Newlyn and St. Ives, offering his services to the artists there.

To this day he cannot understand why no one else has ever wished to paint him.

When *The Brothers* was accepted by the Royal Academy, Joan was quick to say that the success of the picture was due no more to her painting than to the patient and friendly way in which the three brothers who were her models had sat for it. In order that she might finish her work, it had been necessary for one of them to remain motionless with his arms crossed for three hours at a stretch, with the result, so he declared, that he had not been able to sleep for the acute pains in his chest!

When this picture was exhibited, one London critic suggested that all three men in it had been painted from the same model. When Joan called his attention to the difference in their faces, he answered that there was just such a difference as a painter would naturally make, supposing he had painted all three from one sitter. Up to this time Joan had called the picture *The Chequer's Players*. In order that there might be no more misunderstanding, she now changed the name to *The Brothers*.

Joan has had no art training except the criticism of those artists who are friends of the family. She does not keep a sketch book but works directly upon her canvas. When the idea for a picture occurs to her, she jots down the design for it, usually in pencil on a small piece of paper. Then she looks about for her model or models, as the case may be.

When her second picture was accepted by the Royal Academy—*The Concertina Players,* painted when she was sixteen—people interested in the outstanding achievement of young people urged that a collection of her first drawings and painting be published in book form. For they felt, and rightly, that such a group of pictures would be a fascinating record of how a young girl of talent had been able, in eight years, to progress from *Adam and Eve* to *The Concertina Players*. The pictures in this book are the collection thus made.

Since the book was published in England, two years ago, Joan has had a life-size portrait of her brother in the Royal Academy, as well as one entitled *The Little Negress*. And from the time she was fourteen, she has had pictures in all the important Art Exhibitions not only in London and other large cities in England but also in the Paris Salon. And this year she has been elected a full member of the Royal Institute of Oil Painters.

Her present plan is to continue working in much the same manner as she has done, alone and closely studying her subjects. Her ideal—which she has not yet reached—is to stand before an empty canvas and with no preliminary drawing of any kind, begin to lay on the paint that will represent her subject. For she feels that when she is able to do this, she will catch more clearly the beauty of the idea which is in her mind. She wishes to draw so well that she can paint each picture before the glow of its first inspiration has diminished, the beautiful first inspiration which every true artist feels when he glimpses a new creation.

Joan is fortunate in being a member of a family who fully appreciates what it means to be an artist. And she is constantly encouraged to continued effort not only by her own determination but by the steady purpose of her father and mother in their art. For during the years that her pictures have been growing, Joan's father and mother have been receiving widening recognition for their own work, her father for his stories in *The Manchester Guardian,* her mother for her poetry and for her novels, *Hucca's Moor, The Crochet Woman* and *The Growing Trees*. It is interesting, too, to know that while Joan paints portraits of the folk of the Cornish countryside, Ruth Manning-Sanders writes of them.

What is ahead for eighteen-year-old Joan, as she paints on in her studio by the sea? Those who have studied her pictures and her progress predict many things. To Joan herself, these predictions are less important than her own hope—to become the best painter it is in her to be. What if the hours before her easel seem long and wearisome, many a day? What if painting picture after picture after picture will inevitably mean giving up other things which she would enjoy? It will all be worthwhile to her if the pictures that grow beneath her brush are those of which she dreams.

DRAWINGS AND PAINTINGS OF
JOAN MANNING-SANDERS

1. ADAM AND EVE. Done in 1921, at the age of eight. Pastel, 8 by 6 in.

2. THE ISRAELITES MARCHING ROUND THE WALLS OF JERICHO. Done in 1921. Pastel, 15 by 11 in.

3. JOSEPH GOING UP TO BURY HIS FATHER. Done in 1922. Pastel, 15 by 11 in.

4. THE EGYPTIANS PURSUING THE ISRAELITES THROUGH THE RED SEA. Done in 1922. Pastel, 15 by 11 in.

5. KING DAVID DANCING BEFORE THE ARK. Painted in 1923. Water color, 15 by 11 in.

6. THE DEATH OF ABSALOM. Painted in 1924. Water color, 15 by 11 in.

7. ELIJAH AND THE FLAMING ALTAR. Painted in 1924. Water color, 15 by 11 in.

8. A KING FOLLOWING THE STAR OF BETHLEHEM. Painted in 1925 for St. Hilary Church, Cornwall. Water color, 18 by 12 in.

9. THE FLIGHT INTO EGYPT. Painted in 1925 for St. Hilary Church, Cornwall. Water color, 18 by 12 in.

10. AN ANGEL APPEARING TO THE SHEPHERDS. Painted in 1925 for St. Hilary Church, Cornwall. Water color, 18 by 12 in.

11. THE ANNUNCIATION. Painted in 1925 for St. Hilary Church, Cornwall. Water color, 18 by 12 in.

12. THE GLORIFICATION. Painted in 1926 for St. Hilary Church, Cornwall. Water color, 18 by 12 in.

13. THE ADORATION OF THE KINGS. Painted in 1926 for St. Hilary Church, Cornwall. Water color, 18 by 12 in.

14. "DAVID." Drawn in 1925. Pencil, 15 by 12 in.
    [*In the possession of Miss Elizabeth Manning*]

15. "HEATHER." Painted in 1926. Oils, 12 by 10 in.
    [*In the possession of the Artist*]

16. THE PEDLAR. Painted in 1926. Oils, 17 by 15 in.
    [*In the possession of George Manning-Sanders*]

17. DAVID AND THE GLOBE. Painted in 1927. Oils, 22 by 22 in.
   [In the possession of Ruth Manning-Sanders]

18. RAVEN AND SKULL (unfinished). Painted in 1927. Oils, 22 by 20 in.

19. OLD ANDREW. Painted in 1927. Oils, 20 by 18 in.

20. "GRACIE." Painted in 1927. Oils, 30 by 25 in.

21. YOUNG ANDREW. Painted in 1927. Oils, 15 by 12 in.

22. THE BROTHERS. Painted in 1928. Oils, 36 by 34 in.
   [In the possession of Captain Ernest A. Elgee]

23. A PORTRAIT OF HERSELF. Painted in 1928. Oils, 20 by 15 in.

24. THE PLOUGHING MATCH. Painted in 1928. Oils, 30 by 22 in.

25. H. S. COWPER, Esq., J.P., F.S.A. Painted in 1928. Oils, 22 by 17 in.
   [In the possession of H. S. Cowper, Esq.]

26. BERTHA LOUISA. Painted in 1928. Oils, 25 by 17 in.

27. "VELLENDREATH." Painted in 1928. Oils, 12 by 10 in.

28. THE BABY. Painted in 1928. Oils, 22 by 14 in.

29. THE CONCERTINA PLAYERS. Painted in 1929. Oils, 58 by 56 in.
   [In the possession of Sir Woolmer White, Bart.]

30. Detail No. 1 from "The Concertina Players"

31. Detail No. 2 from "The Concertina Players"

32. Detail No. 3 from "The Concertina Players"

DRAWINGS AND PAINTINGS

OF

JOAN MANNING-SANDERS

*Made between the ages of eight
and sixteen years*

I

ADAM AND EVE

Done in 1921

Drawn in colored chalk when Joan was eight
years old

2

THE ISRAELITES MARCHING ROUND
THE WALLS OF JERICHO

Done in 1921

Drawn in colored chalk when Joan was eight
years old, this picture was made after she had
read the Bible story and had studied the costumes of those ancient days

3

JOSEPH GOING UP TO BURY
HIS FATHER

Done in 1922

Before she drew this picture, when she was
nine, Joan and her brother, David, made cardboard models of the Egyptian chariots

And Joseph went up to bury his Father: and with him went up all the servants of Pharaoh, the elders of his house...... And all the house of Joseph, and his brethren......both chariots and horsemen: and it was a very great company

4

THE EGYPTIANS PURSUING
THE ISRAELITES
THROUGH THE RED SEA

Done in 1922

This picture, too, was drawn when Joan
was nine

And the children of Israel went into the midst of the sea upon the dry ground; and the waters were a wall unto them on their right hand and on their left. And the Egyptians pursued, and went in after them, to the midst of the sea.

5

KING DAVID DANCING
BEFORE THE ARK

Painted in 1923

The year Joan was ten, she began to use water
color paints, instead of chalk for her pictures.
The trees here were copied from one outside
the garden of her own home

And David danced before the Lord with all his might; and David was girded with a linen ephod... And as the ark of the Lord came into the City of David, Michal... looked through a window and saw king David leaping and dancing before the Lord.

6

THE DEATH OF ABSALOM
Painted in 1924

In this picture, painted when Joan was eleven,
she first shows her talent for characterization in
the sly expression she gave the mule

And Absalom rode upon a mule, and the mule went under the thick boughs of a great oak, and his head caught hold of the oak, and he was taken up between the heaven and the earth; and the mule that was under him went away.

7

ELIJAH AND THE FLAMING ALTAR
Painted in 1924

Of this picture, painted when she was eleven, Joan says, "I drew the faces out of my head and hated them afterward"

8

A KING FOLLOWING THE STAR
OF BETHLEHEM

Painted in 1925

This is the first of a series of six pictures of the
Childhood of Christ, which Joan painted for
St. Hilary Church, Cornwall, at the request of
Father Bernard Walke. She completed them all
before she was thirteen. The originals, includ-
ing this and the five pictures following, are
now part of a permanent screen in St. Hilary

9

THE FLIGHT INTO EGYPT

Painted in 1925
for St. Hilary Church, Cornwall

10

AN ANGEL APPEARING
TO THE SHEPHERDS

Painted in 1925
for St. Hilary Church, Cornwall

II

THE ANNUNCIATION
Painted in 1925
for St. Hilary Church, Cornwall

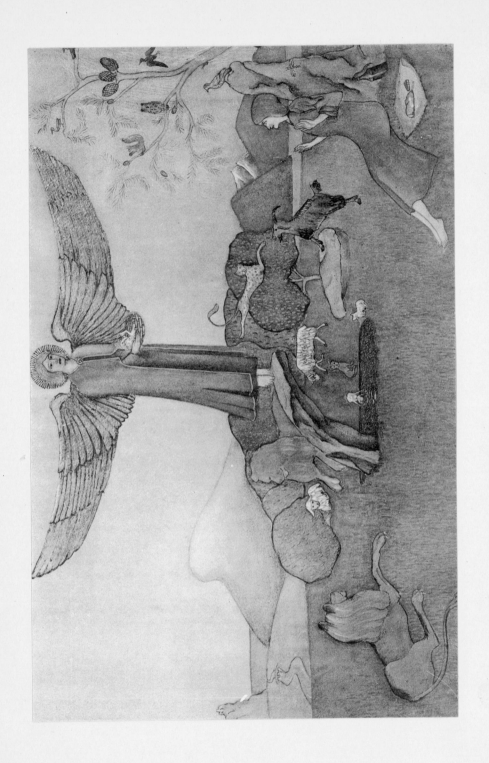

12

THE GLORIFICATION

Painted in 1926
for St. Hilary Church, Cornwall

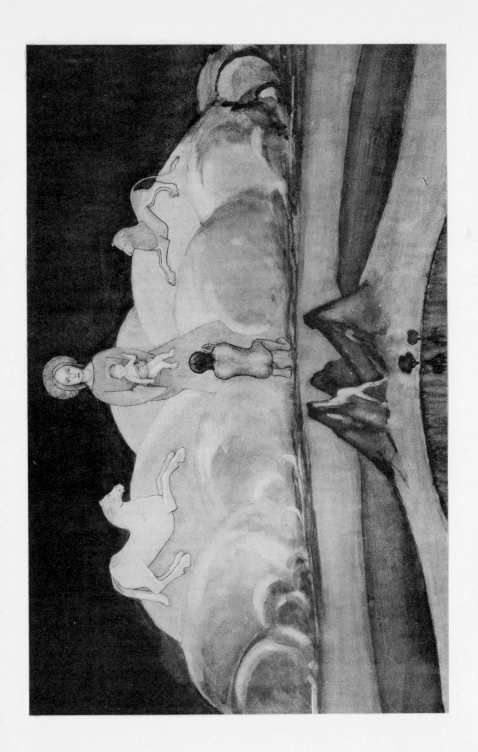

13

THE ADORATION OF THE KINGS

Painted in 1926
for St. Hilary Church, Cornwall

14

"DAVID"

Drawn in 1925

With this sketch of her brother, David, Joan at twelve years of age started her work in realistic portraiture

"DAVID"

By Joan Manning-Sanders

Christmas 1925

15

"HEATHER"
Painted in 1926

"Heather" was one of Joan's first portraits to be done in oils. This portrait, painted when she was thirteen, was completed the year she was given her studio at Sennen Cove

16

THE PEDLAR
Painted in 1926

This portrait, together with the one of David
which follows, was accepted by the Young Artists' Exhibition in London—the first of Joan's
pictures to appear at a public exhibition

DAVID AND THE GLOBE
Painted in 1927

It is interesting to compare this portrait of
David, made the year Joan was fourteen, with
the sketch she drew of him when she
was twelve

18

RAVEN AND SKULL (unfinished)

Painted in 1927

19

OLD ANDREW
Painted in 1927

20

"GRACIE"

Painted in 1927

21

YOUNG ANDREW
Painted in 1927

This picture completes Joan's work done during the first year in her Sennen Cove studio and after her family had decided she might concentrate upon her art. *David and the Globe, Raven and Skull, Old Andrew, "Gracie,"* and *Young Andrew* show how fully she justified that decision

THE BROTHERS
Painted in 1928

This picture, painted the year Joan was fifteen,
was accepted for exhibition at the important
Royal Academy in London. Exhibited side by
side with the work of older, established artists,
it was widely praised by eminent art critics as
the work of a young artist who not only showed
great promise for the future but whose present
achievement was notable

23

A PORTRAIT OF HERSELF
Painted in 1928

24

THE PLOUGHING MATCH

Painted in 1928

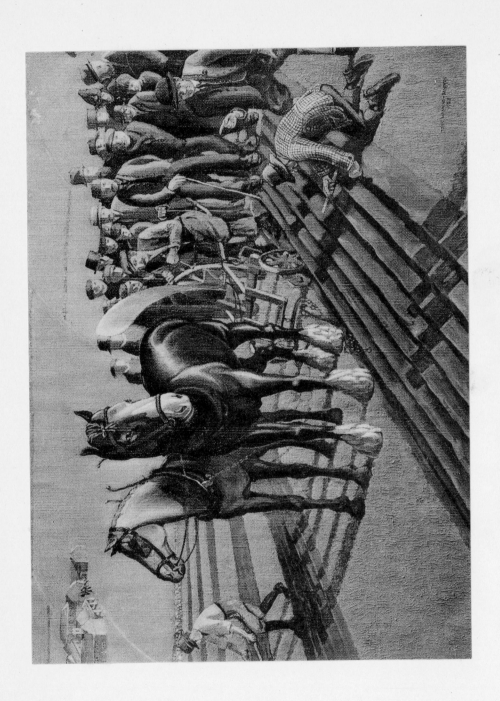

25

H. S. COWPER, Esq., J.P., F.S.A.

Painted in 1928

This was Joan's first commissioned portrait,
painted at Mr. Cowper's own request, the year
she was fifteen

26

BERTHA LOUISA
Painted in 1928

27

"VELLENDREATH"

Painted in 1928

28

THE BABY
Painted in 1928

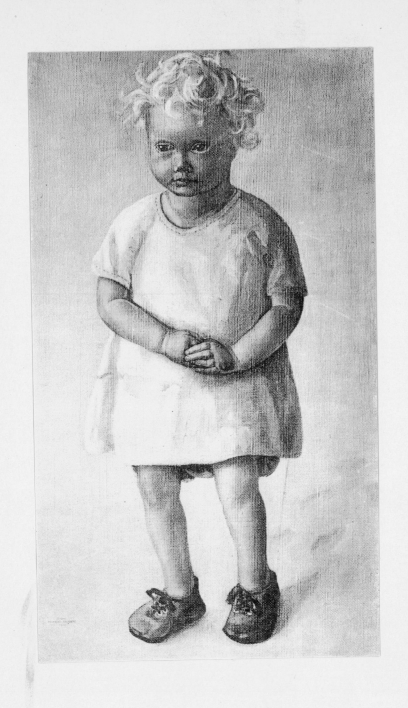

29

THE CONCERTINA PLAYERS

Painted in 1929

This was the second of Joan's pictures to be accepted by the Royal Academy—an honor which has since been annually conferred upon her

30

Detail No. 1 from "The Concertina Players"

31

Detail No. 2 from "The Concertina Players"

32

Detail No. 3 from "The Concertina Players"

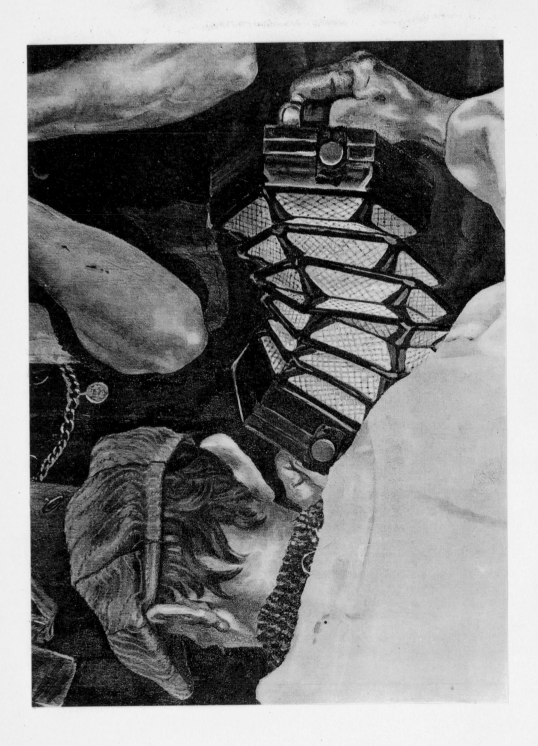